DANCE OF DEATH

DANCE OF DEATH

A
Graphic
Commentary
On
The Danse Macabre
Through
The Centuries
By
FRITZ EICHENBERG

ABBEVILLE PRESS NEW YORK

LIBRARY OF CONGRESS CATALOGING IN PUBLICATION DATA
Eichenberg, Fritz, 1901–
Dance of Death.

1. Eichenberg, Fritz, 1901–
2. Dance of Death. 3. Prints. 4. Drawing.
I. Title.
N7720.E4A4 1983 760'.0446 82-20780
ISBN 0-89659-339-8

ISBN 0-89659-339-8
LIBRARY OF CONGRESS CATALOG CARD NUMBER: 82-20780

Introduction

As we enter life, bawling, protesting, and asserting ourselves, we should be shocked to learn that we are all terminal cases of one sort or another. We carry on more or less mindlessly, as if we could draw on an inexhaustible credit card, trying not to think when the final bill is due. To show good grace when that fateful moment comes is a much admired but rare achievement. We can resort to religion, to philosophy, to drink or drugs, but dance we must to the tune of the great equalizer.

For centuries, from the days of the Black Death to the days of the A-Bomb, artists and poets have bowed in awe and reverence or have thumbed their noses at that supreme ruler of our lives. The artists' efforts, depending on their resources, have taken the form of popular broadsides, primitive cartoons, graffiti, and incidentally have often gained the stature of great art. Artists who have contemplated in their work the many-sided aspects of death, as a scourge or a liberator, a friend or a foe, have often been taken to task for their morbidity.

They were reminded that society expected them to entertain or amuse—as if art was a kind of music hall for the hard-working business man.

Fortunately, any attempt to regiment has always dismally failed —witness the Nazis' outlawing "Entartete Kunst," degenerate art that did not serve the State, or the Soviets' decree to turn art into a political instrument called "Socialist Realism."

The survival of great art in all its forms has proved beyond doubt its value as a catalyst.

The contemplation of Death, in the sublimation of art, constitutes a very healthy affirmation of life, of its daily challenges and obligations to share its joys—as long as life lasts.

List of Illustrations

Fritz Eichenberg
From a Portfolio of Wood Engravings, 1979–80

Apologia

I grew up in an ancient Roman colony, Colonia Claudia Ara Agrippinensis, later called Cologne, filled with relics of the past. The city still houses the bones of The Three Magi and supposedly those of the 11,000 Virgins who were massacred there with their mistress St. Ursula. Three crowns and eleven flames on the city's coat of arms keep their memory fresh. One realizes that for over 2000 years Death has danced through those streets, up to the time of the last war's bombing raids in which hundreds of thousands perished.

When I was a much-brutalized member of the local gymnasium, my class was asked to write an essay on any subject of our choosing. Without prompting, I selected one of Alfred Rethel's engravings, *Der Tod als Freund*, from his famous *Auch ein Totentanz*, created during the turbulent years of the abortive rebellion of 1848 that ended many young lives on the barricades.

My choice was *Death as a Friend* who rings the church bells for the old custodian who has peacefully expired in his armchair near the open window of the belfry.

I must have been about ten years old, but the memory lingers. At least it earned me one of the few As in my school career, followed by years of war, hunger, air raids, and a revolution heartily welcomed but of short duration.

As postwar students, we looked for voices expressing our own black *Galgenhumor*. We memorized Christian Morgenstern's *Galgenlieder*, recited

> *"Marie, mein Henkers Mädel"—*
> *come, kiss my shining pate.*
> *although the kites*
> *picked out my eyes*
> *still, you are kind and noble—*

ALFRED RETHEL, *DEATH AS A FRIEND*, woodcut, 1850

11

Galgenhumor made our lives bearable, even enjoyable. Bert Brecht's *Three Penny Opera*, fashioned after John Gay's *Beggar's Opera*, made a hero of Mackie Messer, the gallant highwayman, walking gaily to the gallows, cheating Death of his glory. It was a howling success on the stage, and in our unheated studios it played incessantly on our shaky gramophones.

In school and in our bourgeois homes, Death was romanticized in poetry and music. Saint-Saëns' *Danse Macabre*, played on the Steinway by my mother and sisters, was my favorite; Schubert's *Erlkönig*, a desperate father racing Death with his dying son in his arms, an easy second. Schumann's salute to Napoleon, the song of *The Two Grenadiers* lying in their graves waiting for the Emperor's return; or *Der Gute Kamerad* shot on the battlefield, gory songs glorifying dying for *Kaiser, König und Vaterland*, were our daily fare.

For some dark reason our young minds accepted this strange mixture of romance and death—for a while! It prepared a nation for war—and later for Hitler.

And war came to us in 1914—after a shot fired in Serajevo. After the first hurrays, victories on all fronts, the first black-bordered announcements: "We regret to announce," the first ration cards, the blockade, hunger and air raids, nights spent in the cellar, and a little boy growing up deprived of his youth. Exodus thanks to Hitler fifteen years later, and hearing from across the ocean the death throes of Colonia Agrippinensis bombed to smithereens by the Allies.

Remembrance of Things Past

Millenia of War and Peace—
and War and Peace again.
An ancient city, ravaged, sacked, and burnt
by tribes and legions, hordes of mercenaries;
city of churches, saints and sinners,
bombed into ashes, soon to rise again.
Two statues have survived that holocaust:
Our Lady mourns her mutilated child,
while Death, the triple-crowned,
remains the watchful victor.

12

MISERERE ET ST-COLUMBA
FELIX COLONIA AGRIPPINENSIS
ANNO DOMINI 1945

Eichenberg ©1980

A Short Picture Essay
on the Dance of Death

The Dance of Death, le Danse Macabre, der Totentanz, La Danca de la Muerte: they earned their names by virtue of their ethnic origin, as a public performance on improvised stages, in courtyards, cemeteries, or churches. The actors danced, sang, played instruments, and cavorted costumed as skeletons. In short, the Dance of Death became entertainment, a generic term. As it gained in popularity it had to find new media to spread its message. The ambulant play was bound to turn into a pictorial representation, a mural, a blockbook, an illumination, a broadside, or into a series of single prints.

Death became a silent actor in sequences showing him as the Supreme Arbiter, choosing his victims regardless of rank or station in life, perhaps the first attempt to create a moving picture. Sometimes Death was shown in single prints or paintings, as the morbid mood struck the artist.

The dialogue between Man and Death may have originated in Indian or Arabic poetry and ultimately found its way into Europe.

In 1194, Hélinant de Froidmont wrote an essay, *Vers sur la Mort*, which may have inspired a succession of artists and writers to devote themselves to that grim theme, most likely with the tacit approval of the Church.

Around 1355 Francesco Traini showed in his fresco at the Pisa Camposanto the confrontation of *The Three Dead and the Three Living*, a dialogue between Death and the Kings of the Earth, representing Power, Beauty, and Wisdom.

They are told: "Whatever you are, we were. Whatever we are, you will be!" It was the time when The Black Death struck Europe, and almost depopulated it.

GUY MARCHANT, *THE THREE LIVING AND THE THREE DEAD*, woodcut, 1485

GUY MARCHANT, *THE THREE LIVING AND THE THREE DEAD*, woodcut, 1485

A series of frescoes painted by an unknown artist in 1424 at the Cemetery of the Holy Innocents in Paris, a *Danse Macabre des Hommes et des Femmes*, no doubt prompted an enterprising Guy Marchant to translate them into popular woodcuts that were copied and published in many editions.

They must have served as a prototype for similar series of the Dance of the Skeletons, which began to appear all over Europe.

One could consider these inexpensively printed semicomic "strips" as popular safety valves, reminders to the high and mighty that Death was no respecter of rank, giving to the common people the satisfaction that their bondage would not last forever. The ever-present gallows, the ravages of war, plague, and famine were their constant reminders of life's fragility, a daily spectacle.

For the highborn, Death was an occasion for pomp and circumstance, celebrated with ceremony and sanctified by the church authorities.

Even executions were public events attended by those in power, prolonged at will by slow torture, especially where heretics were concerned.

The nobility liked its *Book of Hours*, richly illuminated by favorite artists to show that a pious life would lead to a glorious death in the arms of the Church.

The Art of Dying, *Ars Moriendi*, a series of prints showing good and evil, angels and devils fighting for the soul of man, became popular in the 1470's all over the civilized continent, a guideline for those privileged to die in bed.

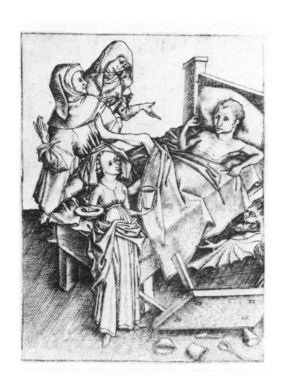 

MASTER E.S., *ARS MORIENDI*, ca. 1470

17

Most of the artists were anonymous, their work often crude and naive. It seems they were liable to borrow freely from each other, as was customary in their time.

But soon we begin to discover more skilled hands and sophisticated minds at work.

We are almost sure that young Albrecht Dürer was responsible for the woodcuts in Sebastian Brant's *Ship of Fools*, perhaps also for those in the Ritter vom Turn's little tract of warning designed to protect his daughter's virtue—lest Death or the Devil would take her!

We may assign Olivier de la Marche's name to the *Chevalier Délibéré*, a blockbook showing a princeling's battle with life and death, and attach Wilhelm Pleydenwurff's name to the dancing skeletons in Hartmann Schedel's *Weltchronick*.

As we enter the 16th century, we are happily facing a plethora of outstanding artists fascinated with that now-familiar theme, Death on the prowl, in either single prints or in sequences.

The list is long and the choice difficult, but the crown should easily go to Hans Holbein the Younger, whose forty-one plates of his *Danse Macabre* (engraved by Hans Lützelburger and first published in Lyons in 1538) are still known the world over and have been freely adapted, recut, etched, and lithographed, most often not to their advantage. Though small in format, they carry a wealth of information about the turbulent time—the Reformation—in which the artist and his contemporaries lived, fought, and worked. Holbein spares neither the Pope nor the Emperor—ending his series as impartially as Death does, with the peasant and the beggar.

JOHANNES VON TEPL, *DER ACKERMANN AUS BÖHMEN*, Bamberg, woodcut, 1461

19

OLIVIER DE LA MARCHE, *LE CHEVALIER DÉLIBÉRÉ*, woodcut, 1483

PLEYDENWURFF, *SCHEDEL'S NUREMBERG CHRONICLE*, woodcut, 1493

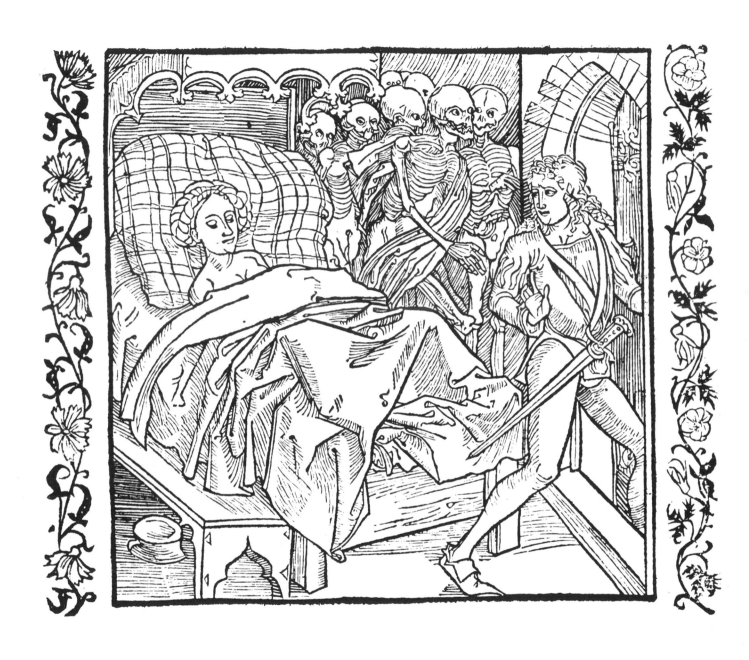

ALBRECHT DÜRER (?), *DER RITTER VOM TURN*, woodcut, 1493 .

22

Mag Adel/gůt/ſterck/jugents zyer
Han fryd vnd růw/o todt vor dir:
Alls das/das leben ye gewann
Vnd tődtlich iſt/das můß dar von

dů blibſt

Nit furſehen den dot
Wir werden ßtrogen ließen fründt
All die vff erden leben ſyndt
Das wir fürſehen nit ßy zyt·
Den ßott/der vnſer doch ſchont nüt

ALBRECHT DÜRER (?), *DAS NARRENSCHIFF* (Sebastian Brant), woodcut, 1494

SAVONAROLA, *PREDICA DELL ARTE DEL BENE MORIRE*, ca. 1496

24

GEILER VON KAISERSBERG, *SERMONES*, woodcut, 1514

25

DANIEL HOPFER, *LOVERS, DEATH, AND DEVIL*, etching, ca. 1520

26

HANS SEBALD BEHAM, *WOMAN AND DEATH AS JESTER*, engraving, 1541

27

URS GRAF, *TWO MERCENARIES, WHORE AND DEATH*, woodcut, 1524

URS GRAF, *WOMAN WITH SKULL AND TWO SUITORS*, woodcut, N.D.

Few of the great artists of his time have dealt with the Dance of Death as thoroughly as Holbein did. But most of them at one time or another have depicted the unwelcome caller in their work. Of course, many of the artists were actively engaged in the battles of the Reformation—and suffered for it. Albrecht Dürer's *Four Horsemen of the Apocalypse* and his *Knight, Death and Devil*, must head the list; they have been shown so extensively that we may dispense with them here. He is followed by Weiditz (known as the Petrarca Master), Aldegrever, and Burgkmair, each great in his own right but somehow overshadowed by Dürer. There is Urs Graf, the artist-mercenary; Hans Baldung Grien, addicted to the supernatural; and those brave artists involved in the Peasant Rebellion who paid a heavy price for their partisanship, among them Niklaus Manuel Deutsch, known for his *Berner Totentanz*, George Pencz, and the valiant brothers Hans Sebald and Bartel Beham, who had sided with the peasants and had looked Death in the eye so often.

Quite out of the ordinary is the physician Vesalius's treatise, *De Humani Corporis Fabrica*, showing strangely animated corpses peeled down to their bones in a most graceful fashion, cut by Stefan von Kalkar. Here, Death is put in his proper place, quite objectively, and made to serve medical science.

HANS HOLBEIN, *DEATH AND PLOWMAN*, woodcut, 1583

31

HANS WEIDITZ, *DEATH AND THE FAMILY*, from *Petrarca's Trostspiegel*, woodcut, 1532

HANS WEIDITZ, *DEATH AND THE KING*, from *Petrarca's Trostspiegel*, woodcut, 1532

33

HANS SEBALD BEHAM, *ADAM, EVE, AND DEATH*, engraving, 1543

34

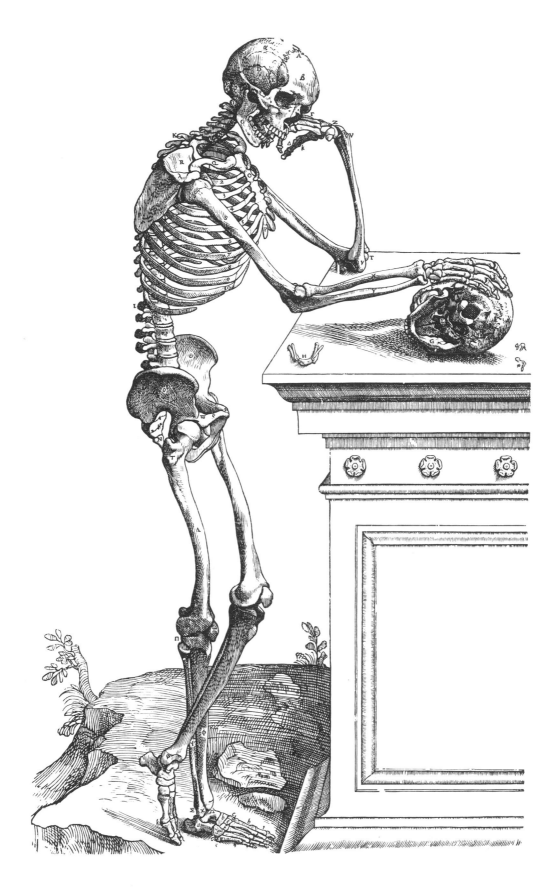

VESALIUS–KALKAR, *DE HUMANI CORPORIS FABRICA*, woodcut, 1543

35

As we enter the Baroque, we see Death assuming an air of flamboyancy, waving a banner and ready to do battle—one seems to hear fife and drum. It is the age of the Thirty Years' War (which lasted almost a hundred—and devastated Europe from one end to the other). Closely observed by Jacques Callot, artist from Lorraine, in his pitiless series of etchings, *Les Misères de la Guerre* showed a dance of death matched by Goya's *Los Desastros de la Guerra* two hundred years later.

Italian flamboyance shows in Agostino Veneziano's *Death and Devil Fighting for a Soul*. We are attending a spirited performance closely related to Mantegna and Pollaiuolo's mastery of the human body.

And we can almost listen to the elegant conversation of two skeletons in Bernardino Genga's *Anatomia*, acting like doctors discussing patients, comparing notes.

In Italy, Stefano Della Bella addressed himself to the theme more allegorically in a series of etchings, *Five Deaths*, somewhat lacking in compassion, while the famous preacher Abraham a Santa Clara raises a warning finger in his *Universal Mirror of Death*, published in 1711 at Nürnberg under the title *Allgemeiner Todtenspiegel*.

In its unsophisticated message it is somewhat similar to several other unremarkable series on the same theme, like the brothers Meyers' large series of etchings entitled, *Sterbenspiegel* and *Ein Totentanz*. Mitelli's *La Vita Humana* is presenting a familiar form of broadside following mankind's inexorable procession from the cradle to the grave.

Michael Rentz, famous for his hunting scenes, goes after human game in his carefully staged *Geistliche Todts-Gedanken*; one is tempted to call his work "Salon Art."

JACQUES CALLOT, *LES MISÈRES ET LES MALHEURES DE LA GUERRE*, three etchings, 1633

37

LA VITA
HVMANA

INFANZIA.

PVERIZIA.

AD

Tetta, pappa, pianti, e cacca.

Scherzi, e trastulli.

Giuochi

Gioi. Mitelli In. F. 1690.

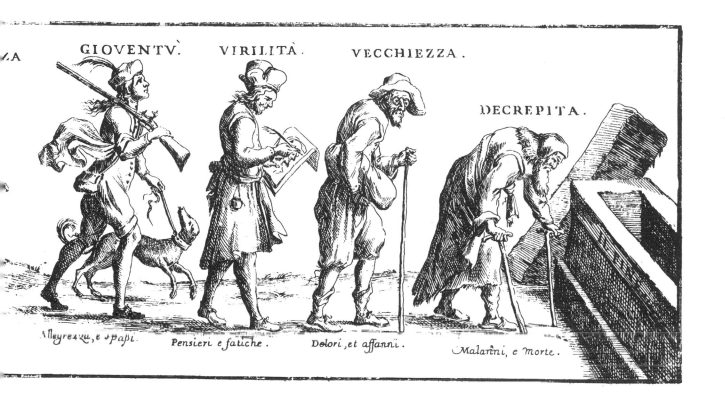

GIOVENTÙ.   VIRILITÀ.   VECCHIEZZA.

DECREPITA.

Allegrezze, e spassi.   Pensieri e fatiche.   Dolori, et affanni.   Malanni, e Morte.

GIUSEPPE MARIA MITELLI, *LA VITA HUMANA*, engraving, 1690

39

AGOSTINO VENEZIANO (after Bandinelli), *DEATH AND DEVIL FIGHTING FOR A SOUL*, engraving, 1518

BERNARDINO GENGA, *ANATOMIA*, engraving, 1691

41

Icy la Mort triomphe entre les funerailles;
Ses plus beaux promenoirs sont les lieux des batailles;
Son Throsne s'affermit de la cheute des morts;
Elle change a l'instant par ses armes subtiles
En riuiere de sang les Campagnes fertiles,
Et les plaines de Mars en montagnes de corps.

Parmi les Escadrons, elle fait des rauages
Du trenchant de sa faux, s'ouure mille passages
Caualiers et Cheuaux tombent egalement,
Et ses coups sont si promps, q'vn puissant corps d'armée
D'vn milion de corps horriblement formée
Semble n'auoir laissé q'vne ame seulement.

Ste. Della Bella in. et fc. Cum Pri. Reg.

STEFANO DELLA BELLA, *THE FIVE DEATHS*, etching, ca. 1660

The 18th century gave birth to the French Revolution and the guillotine, which made short shrift of death in public performances.

But despite the fact that heads were rolling, no great artists came forward to record this Dance of Death in the officially proclaimed Age of Reason. It's a pity that the great William Hogarth confined himself to the moralistic series of the Rake's and the Harlot's Progress.

In England, the promising young artist Richard Newton completed ten etchings for his own Dance of Death, before he died at the age of twenty-one.

In Germany, the gifted Daniel Chodowiecki produced ten engravings for a somewhat bourgeois Dance of Death. The long-forgotten Brothers von Mechel gave image and verse to their Swiss *Todten-Tanz von Basel*. Schellenberg in Winterthur published *Freund Hein*; Johann Nilson and Salomon von Rustingh in Nürnberg gave us *Schauplatz des Todes*, which left no impact on an evidently complacent public.

And, in America, the New Republic? Not much to report: Rembrandt Peale completed a painting, *The Court of Death*, which did not prove to be very popular among the new settlers preoccupied with the struggle for survival.

ABRAHAM A SANTA CLARA, *ALLGEMEINER TODTEN-SPIEGEL*, engraving, 1711

44

DANIEL CHODOWIECKI, *TOTENTANZ*, engraving, 1792

45

MICHAEL RENTZ, *GEISTLICHE TODTS-GEDANKEN*, engraving, 1753

Todt zum Koch.

Komm her Hans Koch du mußt darvon/
Wie bist so feißt/du kanst kaum gohn:
Haft du schon kocht viel süsser Schleck/
Wirt dir jetzund sawr/du must hinweg.

Der Koch.

Ich hab kocht Hüner/Gänß vnd Fisch
Meim Herren viel mal vber Disch/
Wildbret/Bastet vnd Marziban:
O wee meins Bauchs/ich muß darvon.

GEBRÜDER VON MECHEL, *DER TODTEN-TANZ*, engraving, 1796

47

The 19th century began with a volley of shots heard around the world, promising a rich harvest for Death waiting in the wings. The Age of Reason was forgotten—Napoleon was on the march to conquer the world.

Planning the invasion of England, he faced the formidable trio of Thomas Rowlandson, James Gillray, and George Cruikshank, whose great cartoon-etchings sold for pennies as popular prints, and backed the nation's determination to resist the invader with all its strength and courage.

Gillray invented *Little Boney* Bonaparte and bombarded him mercilessly with his barbed prints. Rowlandson, in addition to his political cartoons, poured his gall and humor into his unforgettable *English Dance of Death*, a collection of seventy-two color etchings, published by Ackermann in two volumes in 1815/16.

Goya witnessed the French Invasion of Spain and recorded "man's inhumanity to man" in his own powerful version of a Dance of Death—*Los Disastros de la Guerra*, published after his own death but retaining validity and impact for all time as great works of art as well as invaluable historic documents.

Honoré Daumier, twenty years old when Goya died in exile, took up the battle for the French Republic. Among his four thousand lithographs, we see Death synonymous with war; his other targets: the monarchy, injustice, and the foibles of his countrymen.

THOMAS ROWLANDSON, *NAPOLEON FACING DEATH*, etching, 1814

THOMAS ROWLANDSON, *THE ENGLISH DANCE OF DEATH*, etching, 1815–16

FRANCISCO GOYA, *NADA, ELLO DIRÁ*, from *Los Desastres de la Guerra*, aquatint, 1810–20

FRANCISCO GOYA, *LAS CAMAS DE LA MUERTE*, from *Los Desastres de la Guerra*, aquatint, 1810–20

HONORÉ DAUMIER, *LA PAIX*, lithograph, 1871

HONORÉ DAUMIER, *THE INVENTOR'S DREAM (Le Fusil Chassepot)*, lithograph, 1866

There was much to fight for, with art and with more lethal weapons, and great artists joined the battle.

Death took no holiday. Europe was swept by revolutionary spirits everywhere, and 1848 was the crucial year. Alfred Rethel celebrated it with his seven disillusioned engravings, *Auch ein Totentanz*. Grandville expressed himself in a more bourgeois way in his series, *Voyage pour l'Eternité*. Felicien Rops mixed Eros, Death and Decay in his seventeen prints for a *Danse Macabre*. His *Order Reigns in Warsaw* still speaks strongly to our time. To James Ensor, skeletons were always familiar companions. He showed himself as one of them in his *Self-Portrait 1960*. He died eleven years before that date, a good eighty-nine years old!

The German Max Klinger's highly romanticized series of etchings *Vom Tode* are period pieces, similar to the typically French *Danse Macabre* by Albert Besnard, significantly called *Elle*. A claim to greatness could be made for a simple Mexican whom Diego Rivera called "as great as Goya or Callot." Posterity will judge, but José Guadalupe Posada certainly was a witness to his time and to his people fighting for freedom. His cartoons and his *calaveras*, cut in wood or metal, can be considered a Mexican Dance of Death, still celebrated even now on the Day of the Dead, when everyone munches the familiar skeletons made of sugar, and a festive air prevails in the streets.

ALFRED RETHEL, *DEATH THE VICTOR*, from *Auch ein Totentanz*, I. wood engraving, 1848–49

ALFRED RETHEL, *ON THE BARRICADE*, from *Auch ein Totentanz*, II. wood engraving, 1848–49

GRANDVILLE, *VOYAGE POUR L'ETERNITÉ*, from *Première Etape*, lithograph, ca. 1830

FÉLICIEN ROPS, *L'ORDRE RÈGNE A VARSOVIE!*, lithograph, 1863

PAUL ALBERT BESNARD, *THE END OF IT ALL*, from *Elle*, etching, 1900

FERDINAND BARTH, *DIE ARBEIT DES TODES*, woodcut, 1866

MAX KLINGER, *VOM TODE*, etching, 1898

THOMAS NAST, *MILITARY GLORY*, from *Harper's Weekly*, wood engraving, 1870

ALPHONSE LEGROS, *THE PEOPLE'S WAR*, etching, 1900

RODOLPHE BRESDIN, *THE COMEDY OF DEATH*, etching transferred to lithograph, 1822–85

EDVARD MUNCH, *MAIDEN AND DEATH*, etching, 1864

JAMES ENSOR, *MY PORTRAIT IN 1960*, etching, 1886

JAMES ENSOR, *SKELETONS DISPUTING BEFORE A HANGED MAN*, oil painting, 1891

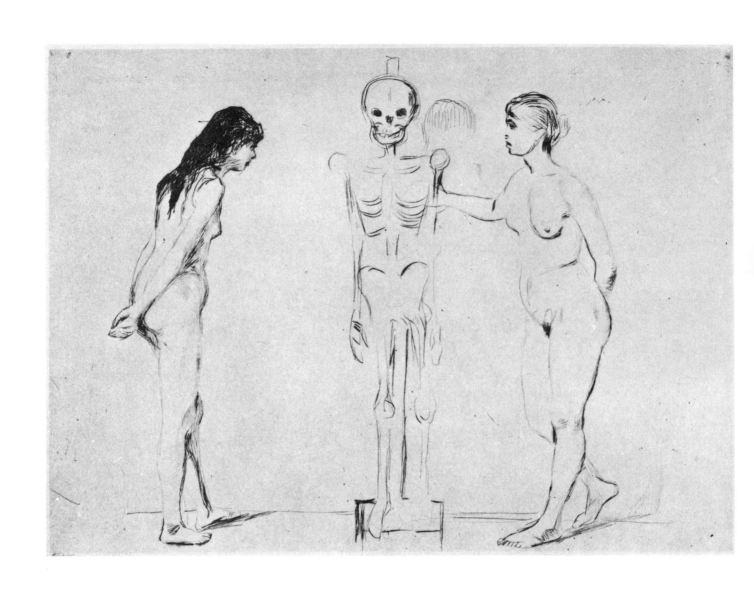

EDVARD MUNCH, *TWO NUDES AND DEATH*, etching, ca. 1894

GUADALUPE POSADA, *CALAVERA OF DON QUICHOTE*, leadcut, N.D.

As we move into our own macabre 20th century so full of war and violence, we might wonder why the theme of Death has not attracted more artists who have witnessed its increasingly senseless, cruel progress. To read between the lines of our history books might have a shocking and salutary effect on our dim memories.

We began the century with the Opium War and the Boxer Rebellion, brutally put down by the Western powers. There were pogroms and a failed revolution in Russia; the Sino-Russian War; wars in the Balkans; rebellions in Africa and India; the first World War, followed by revolutions and the rise of Hitler; the death camps in Germany and the gulags in Russia; Hiroshima and an uneasy peace of short duration; the Viet Nam War (remember My Lai) and its aftermath in Southeast Asia; and the wave of terrorism, abductions, torture, and executions; crime in the streets, the drug scene, and nuclear and other deadly pollutions—the list is long and there is no end in sight. In colloquial English: Death never had it so good!

Living on the fringe of society, rarely being taken very seriously, artists and poets have developed a special sensitivity, a different perspective concerning the world's ills and the human condition. They act as our prophets—rarely heeded—more often laughed at and ignored.

Death is a living presence. We see him in so many self-portraits of artists of our time, looking over their shoulders, smiling, waiting, biding his time.

BLIX, *DEATH IN FLANDERS*, drawing from *Simplicissimus*, 1917

We may remember the self-portraits of Max Beckmann, Lovis Corinth, of Edvard Munch, Max Slevogt, and others of that post-Impressionist period. But we can never forget Käthe Kollwitz's mothers trying to protect their children from early death. Her series of etchings *Die Weber* shows the desperate struggle of the Silesian weavers in which Death is the victor. Her later lithographic sequences she called *Vom Tode*, a powerful Dance of Death, fortunately completed before the Nazis silenced her. But her work always will speak for her with undiminished force and conviction, a mother mourning her children.

Of her generation, perhaps the strongest Totentanz is Otto Dix's suite of twenty-four aquatints called *Der Krieg*. It is an outraged eyewitness report of an artist who suffered through and survived the first World War, the war of the trenches filled with mutilated pieces of humanity, skulls grinning horribly while poppies grow out of their eyesockets. It is a Goyaesque "j'accuse."

George Grosz showed prophetically Death stalking the streets of pre-Hitler Germany. His Death is everywhere in a decaying society, best shown in his major work, *The Face of the Ruling Class*. Not even a skeleton is draft exempt!

Perhaps the German predilection contemplating death as a tangible presence, acts strongly in the work of the Expressionists, the artists usually connected with the Brücke and Blue Rider group of nonconformists. We show here just two examples of their famous exponents, E. L. Kirchner and Emil Nolde. An American art critic, reviewing the recent Expressionist exhibit at the Guggenheim Museum, focused on the *Angst* complex he discovered in much of the work shown. I would rather attribute the preoccupation with death to the European tradition of the Danse Macabre theme going back to the Dark Ages.

E. L. KIRCHNER, *SELF-PORTRAIT WITH DANCING DEATH*, woodcut, 1918

EMIL NOLDE, *PATIENT, DOCTOR, DEATH, AND DEVIL*, etching, 1911

LOVIS CORINTH, *DER KÜNSTLER UND DER TOD*, etching, N.D.

KÄTHE KOLLWITZ, *DEATH*, from *The Weavers*, etching, 1897

KÄTHE KOLLWITZ, *DEATH REACHES FOR A CHILD*, lithograph, 1934–35

75

OTTO DIX, *WAR, (The Wounded)*, aquatint, 1924

OTTO DIX, WAR, *(Seen at Hill Before Cléry-sur-Somme)*, aquatint, 1924

GEORGE GROSZ, *FINIS*, from *Interregnum*, drawing, ca. 1936

GEORGE GROSZ, *I WAS ALWAYS PRESENT*, from *Interregnum*, drawing, ca. 1936

Alfred Kubin's entire work has the foreboding quality of doom and impending death. His *Totentanz* sums up the testament of a haunted soul, in the best pre-Hitler tradition.

In France, prompted by Ambroise Vollard, Georges Rouault spent a decade of his life on his grandiose cycle of fifty-eight etchings *Miserere et Guerre*. It is in equal parts a Dance of Life and Death, but clearly Faith and Redemption prevail. The etchings were published in 1926, in the aftermath of the first World War.

Stretching a point, Picasso's *Guernica* might be called a requiem for a little Spanish community, wiped out by Death from the air. Even his cartoon-like etchings, *The Dream and Lie of Franco*, have the fury of a medieval Danse Macabre, bloody tears for the rape of his native country.

The same black rage shows in the Danse Macabre of the Mexican Jean Charlot and the Flemish Frans Masereel, artists with a deep feeling for the injustices inflicted on the living masses with whom they identified.

The Argentinian-born Mauricio Lasansky created perhaps the most powerful Dance of Death of our time in his *Nazi Drawings*, published in 1966. It is a savage indictment of organized death in Nazi uniform, burned into our memories with relentless rage and great artistry.

ALFRED KUBIN, *TOTENTANZ*, drawing, 1915–16

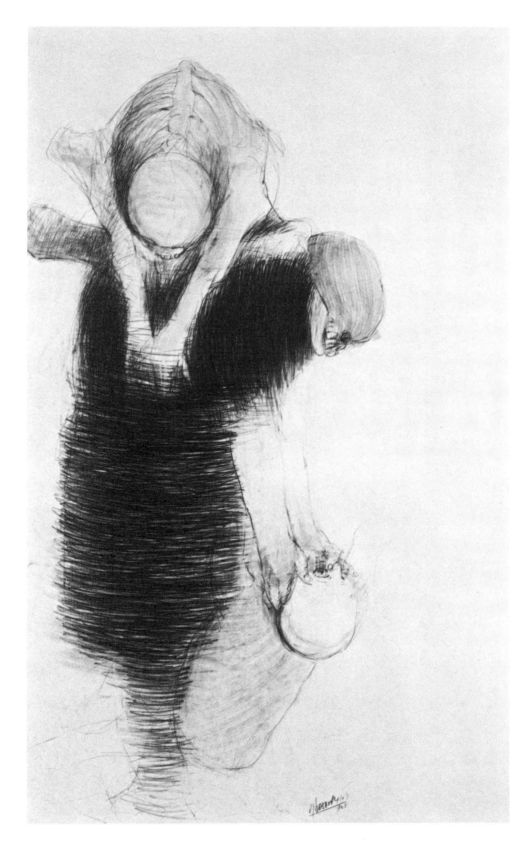

MAURICIO LASANSKY, No. 14 of *THE NAZI DRAWINGS*, 1961–66

MAURICIO LASANSKY, No. 17 of *THE NAZI DRAWINGS*, 1961–66

GEORGES ROUAULT, *DEBOUT LES MORTS,* from *Miserere et Guerre*, etching, 1916–27

GEORGES ROUAULT, *CE SERA LA DERNIÈRE, PETIT PÈRE!*, from *Miserere et Guerre*, etching, 1916–27

Hap Grieshaber's forty powerful woodcuts are based on the *Totentanz von Basel*, inspired originally by the Black Death of 1439. Five hundred years have passed but the German artist's adaptations now speak strongly to our condition.

More conventional is his countryman A. Paul Weber's *Totentanz*, full of the nightmares of war and Nazi brutality.

Three thousand miles away, Robert Rauschenberg created several collage prints commemorating death in our time, one of the few notable American artists to do so. One print, simply called *Signs*, consists of a montage of all of the well-known victims that Death collected arbitrarily in the 1960s, from the Kennedys to Martin Luther King, with Janis Joplin providing the requiem for the victims of the Viet Nam War.

Federico Castellon, a Spanish-American, built up steadily a major and lasting oeuvre, from his early surrealist period to his last great series of sixteen lithographs for E. A. Poe's *The Mask of the Red Death*, indeed Castellon's own Danse Macabre. It was finished in Paris at the Atelier Desjobert a few years before his untimely death.

Antonio Frasconi, Uruguayan-American artist whose work is deeply committed to the social and political issues of our time, created a memorable series of woodcuts during the height of the Viet Nam War called *The Hawks*—Death in the shape of much-decorated birds of prey.

But perhaps the most moving graphic documents on the Holocaust came out of a portfolio of twenty-four drawings by a former Auschwitz inmate, George Zielezinski, drawn right after the Liberation in 1946.

Ernst Wiechert, German poet, who survived the same man-made hell, writes in his introduction to this Dance of Death:

> *"Some will turn away with a curse, some with*
> *a prayer—and some with tears . . . !"*

86

HAP GRIESHABER, *THE QUEEN*, from *Totentanz von Basel*, woodcut, 1968

A. PAUL WEBER, *THE MASTER OF THE WALL*, from *Critical Calendar*, lithograph, 1965

FEDERICO CASTELLON, *THE MASK OF THE RED DEATH*, by E. A. Poe, lithograph, 1969

FRANS MASEREEL, *THAT IS NO DREAM*, from *Totentanz*, drawing, 1917–20

FRANS MASEREEL, *TOTENTANZ 1940*, drawing

ANTONIO FRASCONI, *THE HAWKS*, woodcut, 1966

92

JEAN CHARLOT, *DANCE OF DEATH*, drawing, 1961

GEORGE ZIELEZINSKI, *SHADOWS ON THE PARADE GROUND*, from *Images of Horror*, drawing, 194

GEORGE ZIELEZINSKI, *THE HOSPITAL*, from *Images of Horror*, drawing, 1943

PICASSO, *DREAM AND LIE OF FRANCO, January 8–9, and June 7, 1937,* aquatint, 1937

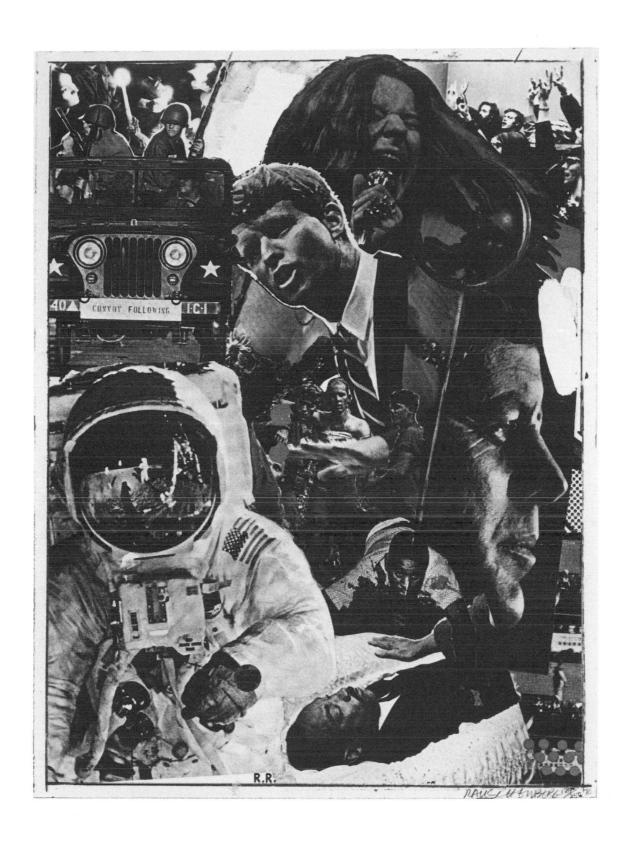

ROBERT RAUSCHENBERG, *SIGNS*, photo-silkscreen, 1970

97

The Artist
on His Own Behalf

This short survey of such a vast panorama of art and history cannot possibly claim to be complete. At this moment, new skeletons may hit the stage. These preceding images may serve, at some risk, as a curtain raiser for my own obsession with a great theme that cannot be ignored.

It also gives this artist an opportunity to pay homage to the great masters who have inspired him. I discovered with Goya that "man is man's most cruel enemy," and that Death, if faced squarely, often can be considered a most compassionate friend. Each period of history produces its witnesses—and the image-makers seem to be the most persistent and incorruptible among them, never to be forgotten.

These prints address themselves to the most burning social and political issues of our time. They hope to speak for a multitude of concerned people.

DANCE OF DEATH

Seventeen Wood Engravings by Fritz Eichenberg

The Ship of Fools

Foul weather for The Ship of Fools,
the sails are gone, the winds are blowing,
the waves are higher than a kite.
Despite it all those fools are fighting—
who knows what for?
Only the Captain keeps his cool and grins—
he knows who wins!

Saturday Night Special

We have a special on Saturday night!
Step in, my boys, the price is right.
We'll give you an extra bonus as well
with all expenses paid—
a weekend trip to Hell.

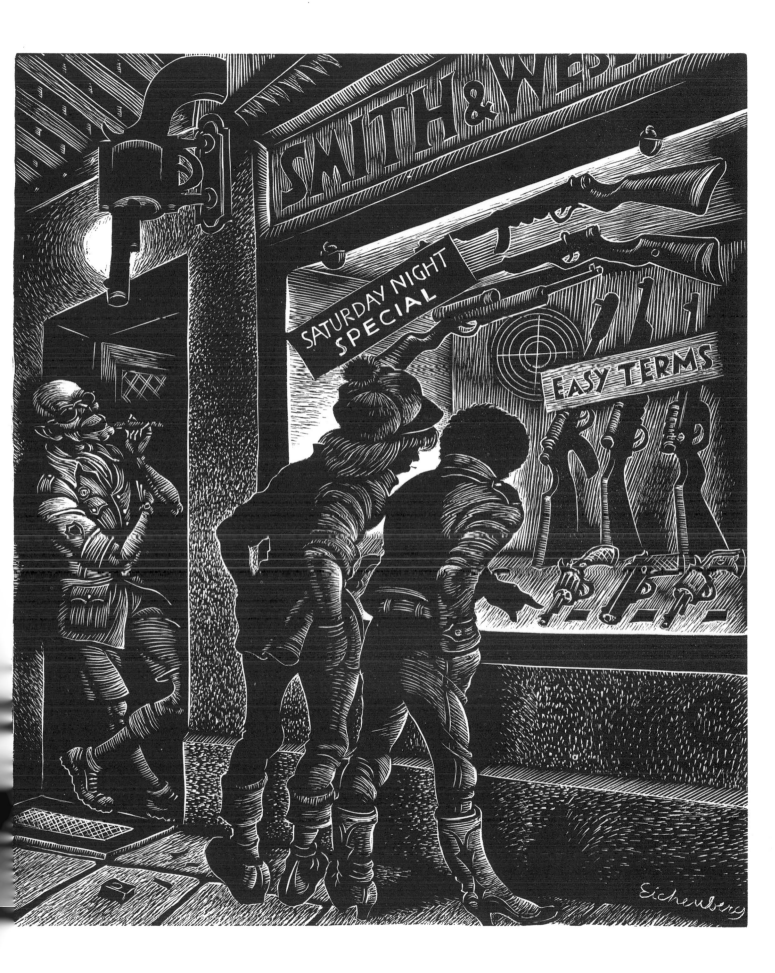

The Pimp

The pimp surveys his beat.
"Not bad," he smiles, "despite recession—
a lot of luscious flesh for sale.
Those suckers know it's tainted,
that I bet,
but then, they get a souvenir
they won't forget."

The Last Rehearsal

"Remember, dear, those halcyon days,
the rave reviews, the rose bouquets,
the curtain calls that never stopped?
My eyes get weak, the mirror fades,
I trust in you, my faithful friend,
to stay with me until the end."

The Angels Are Coming

The Angels are roaring into town
you better let your shutters down.
Boys will be boys and want to have their fun.
But, brother, watch your step,
since you can never tell
when good clean fun
may turn into a blazing hell.

The Last Cocktail

A Bloody Mary or a Mickey Finn,
a reefer or some coke—
it blurs the pain of existential living.
What if it's temporary? So is life.
"I'm smashed—I'm stoned—I'm tight—
my shrink says—oops, I'm sorry—
What fun! See you, maybe, tomorrow!"

Child Care Center

Give us your kids, we'll take good care of them.
They like to play—we give them toys
to blast each other off the map.
"Freedom and Brotherhood"—bang bang—
"The Right to Live"—bang—you're dead again.
We'll match you bomb for bomb
to make a better world for our darling kids—
if they should live that long.

Death Row

Who gave us power
over life and death?
Are we omniscient
godlike creatures
pure of heart
who may decree
who's worth to live or die?
Killing is wrong
no matter in whose name
it's done.

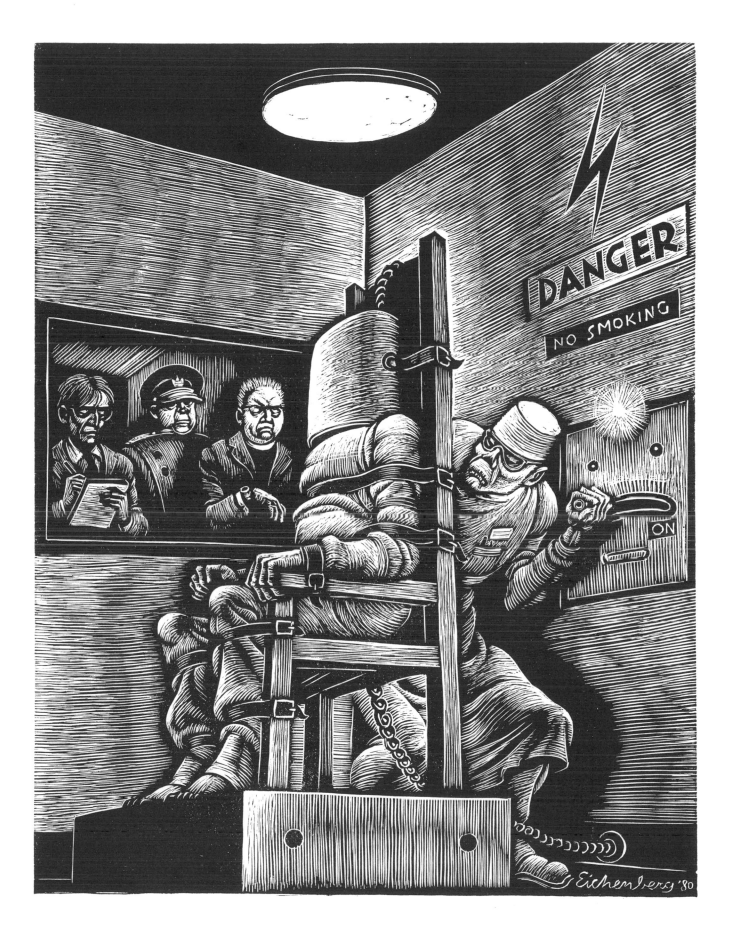

To Learn a Trade

"We want you, son, to learn a trade
and all the useful things you need
in the Pursuit of Happiness
as guaranteed in our Constitution.
In this pursuit, of course,
it may be necessary
to kill your fellow man, or, glory be,
be killed yourself and so become a hero.
Sign on the dotted line,
my friend, and you'll be mine!"

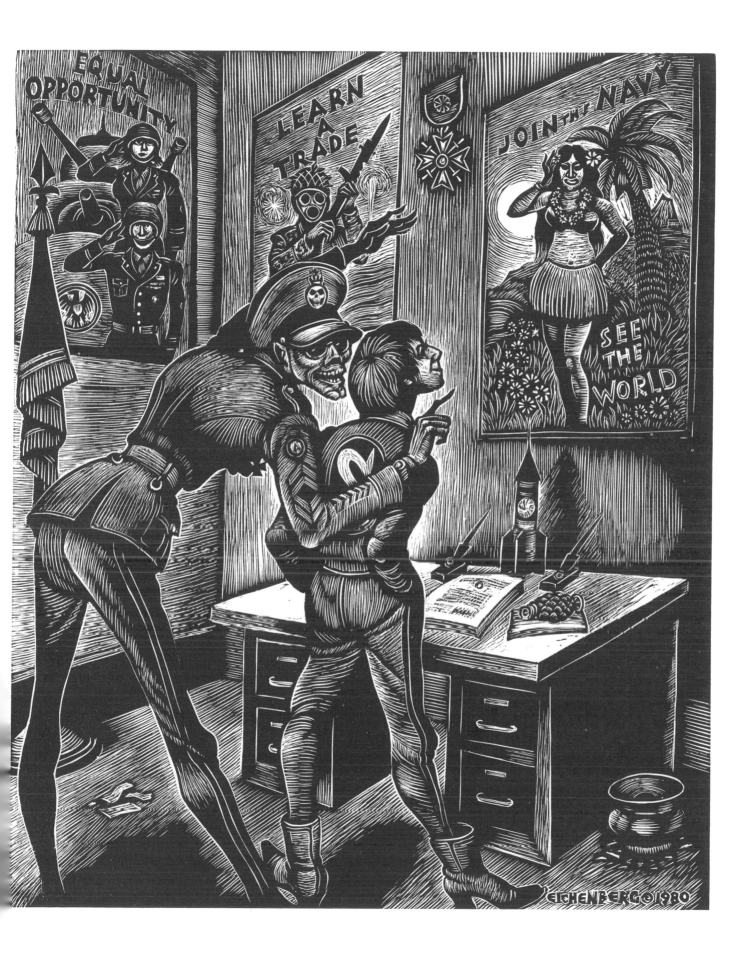

The Crucifixion

And as they nailed Him to the Cross
on which was written INRI —
JESUS OF NAZARETH, KING OF THE JEWS,
He said, "Father forgive them
for they know not what they do."
And at the hour of his death he cried:
"My God, why hast thou forsaken me?"

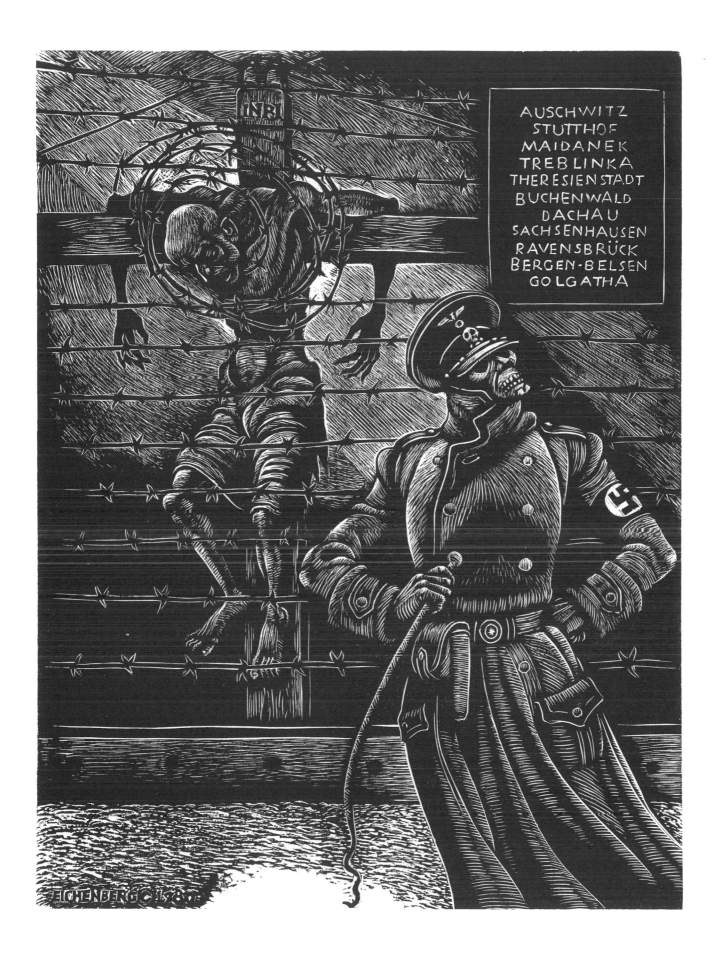

The Refugees

Tossed by the winds of war and violence
they are dispersed across the Earth,
despised, unwanted, famished,
torn from the lands they love.
Eternal pilgrims until Death, the Merciful,
will take them home.

The Last Shot

Yes, Man, I know
the dice are loaded!
So what?
Life is a gamble anyhow!
You have a choice
to be or not to be,
to shoot, snort, smoke
for kicks or nightmares,
for heaven or for hell.
Who cares!
Who cares?

Stalemate

The stakes are high.
Armed to their grinning teeth
they play for keeps
and knowing all the tricks
they take their time.
Only the weapons change
over the centuries.
Who'll stop the game?

The Watchmen

Death is a busy man—we know.
But he can wait a thousand years
in hidden caves, watching the drums
of deadly waste leaking their stuff
ever so slowly into good Mother Earth.
Yes, Death is patient but somehow
he'll manage to present his bill
to our kids—millennia from now.

The Last Resort

The Golden Age, a well-earned rest,
from a long life of toil and tears.
The sun is setting on the just
who line the benches, swapping tales.
The well-dressed stranger smiles
and listens patiently, though, I'm sure,
he must have heard these tales before.

Weep No More

Someone has pushed the button
and the end has come.
No visible survivors
among the smoking ruins—
except a lonely penitent
in a monk's garb.
He for the first time weeps,
bemoans the final desolation.
No one to talk to—
no more work to do.

FRITZ EICHENBERG was born in Cologne, where he first studied at the School of Applied Arts, then served as a lithographic apprentice at the publishing house of DuMont Schauberg, before being accepted as a master student by Prof. Steiner-Prag at the Academy of Graphic Arts in Leipzig. Moving to Berlin in 1923, he became a roving reporter and staff artist for the Ullstein publishing house until Hitler came to power in 1933, the year that the artist decided to start a new life in the U.S.A. at the height of the Great Depression. He taught at the New School for Social Research in New York, worked on the Federal Art Project, did political cartoons for *The Nation*, and illustrated children's books.

Then came the first important commissions from the Limited Editions Club and the Heritage Press. With wood engravings and lithographs, his favorite media, he illustrated many of the great classics by Dostoevsky and Tolstoy, Turgenev and Pushkin, Swift and Shakespeare.

He became well known for his prints and illustrations for new editions of Edgar Allan Poe, of *Wuthering Heights* and *Jane Eyre* by the Brontë sisters, of the stories by Dylan Thomas and Wilkie Collins.

Many of these prints are now in the permanent collection of the Library of Congress, the National Gallery, the Metropolitan Museum, Yale University Library, the Hermitage, the Vatican, the Bibliothèque Nationale, and many other important public and private collections here and abroad.

Eichenberg started teaching at Pratt Institute in 1947, where he served as chairman of the Art Department and as director of the Pratt Graphics Center, acted as editor-in-chief of *Artist's Proof*, a journal on printmaking, and founded the ADLIB Press.

In 1966 he moved to Rhode Island as chairman of the Art Department of the University in Kingston, resigning his position in 1971. He has traveled extensively in semi-official capacities, to the USSR for the State Department, to Southeast Asia for the J.D.R. III Fund, and has received four honorary degrees of Doctor of Fine Arts between 1972 and 1978, and the Rhode Island Governor's Art Award in 1981.

He has written a definitive work on the graphic arts, *The Art of the Print* (Harry N. Abrams, Inc.); a monograph, *The Wood and the Graver* (Clarkson N. Potter, Inc.); and *Endangered Species and Other Fables with a Twist* (Stemmer House, Inc.), which was nominated for a National Book Award in 1980.

The Limited Editions Club has published Grimmelshausen's *The Adventures of Simplicissimus* with eighteen engravings, and Dostoevsky's *House of the Dead* with ten engravings, printed from the original woodblocks, in 1982, to be followed by Dylan Thomas's *Rebecca's Daughters* (New Directions) and Carl Sandburg's *Rainbows Are Made*, with seven engravings (Harcourt Brace Jovanovich).

In the works are *Beachcomber's Bestiary*, a picture book on strange objects found on the beach, and extensive plans on a pictorial autobiography, to be completed in 1983.

All of the illustrations by Fritz Eichenberg
were originally engraved on Swiss Pearwood, and
are also available to collectors in a special signed
edition of fifty, printed from the 9 x 12 inch
original woodblocks on Mohawk Superfine
softwhite archival paper.
The type was set by Martin Typographers in
Linotype Sabon, originally designed by Jan Tschichold.
The paper was made at the Glatfelter papermill in
Spring Grove, Pennsylvania, and the book
was printed by the Murray Printing Company at Westford,
Massachusetts, and bound in Kingston Natural cloth,
in the spring of 1983.
The endpapers are Strathmore Grandee in Barcelona Gray.
The book was designed by Antonie Eichenberg.

Picture credits

The Ashmolean Museum, Department of Western Art, Oxford, England: p. 17; The Beinecke Rare Book and Manuscript Library, Yale University, New Haven, Connecticut: p. 49 (top); Courtesy Leo Castelli Gallery, New York: p. 97; The Metropolitan Museum of Art, New York: p. 27 (Gift of Mrs. Henry L. Moses), pp. 31, 53 (Rogers Fund); The Museum of Modern Art, New York: p. 67 (Inter-American Fund), p. 73 (Gift of J. B. Neumann), pp. 76, 77 (Gift of Abby Aldrich Rockefeller), p. 85 (Gift of the Artist), p. 96 (Gift of Mrs. Stanley Resor); The Museum of Fine Arts, Boston, Massachusetts: p. 42 (Gift of Mrs. Charles Gaston Smith's Group), p. 64 (top); National Gallery of Art, Washington, D.C.: pp. 37, 50, 51, 52 (Rosenwald Collection); New York Public Library: pp. 11, 34, 40, 71, 72, 84 (Astor, Lenox and Tilden Foundations); Oslo Kommunes Kunstsamlinger, Munch-Museet/Munchforlaget: p. 66; William Benton Museum of Art, University of Connecticut, Storrs: p. 74; Yale Center for British Art, Yale University, New Haven, Connecticut: p. 49 (bottom).